Also by Leslie Scrase: ·

COPING WITH DEATH

A book for the bereaved and those who try to help them.

New Third Edition

Leslie Scrase

UNITED WRITERS
Cornwall

UNITED WRITERS PUBLICATIONS LTD
Ailsa, Castle Gate, Penzance, Cornwall.

British Library Cataloguing in Publication Data:
A catalogue record for this book is
available from the British Library.

ISBN 9781852001353

First published in 1990
Second edition 1996
Reprinted 2002

Third edition copyright © 2008 Leslie Scrase

Printed in Great Britain by
United Writers Publications Ltd
Cornwall.

To the memory of Karuna Anne.

The Author

The author conducted his first ceremony, a Sunday service in a small chapel in North Devon, when he was 17 years old. When this edition comes out, he will have been conducting ceremonies of one kind or another for 60 years. He became a minister of religion, serving in various parts of this country and in South India over a period of about 20 years.

Loss of religious faith took him to the British Humanist Association and the conduct of Humanist ceremonies from the late 1970s until now. He sees himself as no more than a voice, attempting to enable people to achieve the kind of ceremony they desire. Inevitably this involves a good deal of flexibility and openness.

For many years now he has conducted over a hundred ceremonies a year and in recent years this has risen to over 150 a year which suggests that there is a need for celebrants to take this kind of approach.

Twice married, he and Wendy share six children and a host of grandchildren scattered through the south of England.

Preface

When I was still a minister of religion, one of my colleagues was the Revd. Clement Pugsley. A genuine pastor, he had written a small book called *In Sorrows Lone Hour*. It was that book which led me to try to provide a book for people with no real religious faith.

The kindness of a Finnish friend and publisher, Markku Vartiainen got the first edition off the ground and the use made of the book by the British Humanist Association helped to ensure a further edition and reprintings.

As I draw near to the end of my working life, demand for this book leads me to a third and final edition. I am grateful to Malcolm Sheppard of United Writers Publications who has served me so well in the past with the publication of *An Evacuee*, *A Prized Pupil!*, and *A Reluctant Seaman* and who now takes this book under his wing for me.

Leslie Scrase

Contents

Introduction

In the course of my lifetime I have seen great poverty and hardship. I have seen disease at its most destructive. I have had the privilege of living with people through the most desolating experiences of life. I have spent a good deal of time with those who were dying and with those who have been bereaved. And of course, I have lost loved ones of my own – among them a child, a brother, a nephew and intimate friends who all died young.

It may seem boastful to begin in this way but I have nothing to boast about. I mention these things in an attempt to show that I am not altogether unqualified to write this book. Perhaps I should add that I have conducted a very large number of funerals. There is nothing special about all this. It is simply the way my path of life has carried me.

Death and bereavement are part of our universal human experience. These are things we all have to face. Some face them supported by their religious beliefs. I have often heard such people say, 'I don't know how I could have coped without my faith.' I can only say that many of us have no such beliefs and cope perfectly well without them.

I would venture to hope that this book might be of use to religious people, but it is written primarily for those who live their lives on the assumption that this is the only life we have: atheists, agnostics, humanists, rationalists and sceptics. In part one of the book I consider some of the things people need to know and some of the things it may be useful to think about.

In part two there are a number of passages which I have found of value at one time or another. Among these most people will find something that matches their own situation, their own feelings or needs. It is from these that most comfort will be derived by those who are facing sorrow's lonely hours.

There is something very special about being allowed to share in the intimate moments of other people's lives but the experience is also emotionally very costly. Grief-stricken people need to be able to draw on our resources as well as on their own.

Sadly it sometimes works the other way round. A man once said to me, 'Don't bring me sympathy. It's weakening.'

He was right. There are comforters who sap our resources and leave us drained. But there is also a kind of sympathy which is supportive and which brings us strength and solace. With or without that support, again and again in my lifetime I have seen the human spirit rise from the depths and triumph over the worst that life can bring.

If this book is of the slightest help in achieving that kind of triumph it will have achieved its purpose.

Leslie Scrase

Part One:

Practical and Philosophical

I. Call the Funeral Director

When a loved one dies we are often distracted beyond words. We don't know what to do.

As long as there was life there were things that we could do even if we were only sitting by someone's bedside. But now that they have gone even that last ministry of companionship is meaningless and we feel totally lost.

Perhaps the first thing to do is to make yet another 'good cup of tea'. The second is to call the undertaker or funeral director.

We can safely leave most things in his hands. He will know what has to be done. Some things he will do himself. Others he will leave to us – but he will tell us what we have to do and how to go about it.

When it comes to the funeral arrangements he will want to know whether we want a burial or a cremation. He will also ask what sort of clergyman we want. It is at this point that we need to make it clear if we want to create and conduct the ceremony ourselves. Alternatively we may want a humanist ceremony with a humanist celebrant.

Although more and more undertakers are aware of the existence of secular organisations and are in touch with celebrants in their own areas, there are still some who need our direction. They can be pointed to any of the national humanist organisations such as the British Humanist Association, the Association of Humanist Celebrants, The Rationalist Press Association, The National Secular Society or (for people in the

London area) the South Place Ethical Society.

If we wish to conduct the funeral ourselves we should do so. All we need to remember is to keep the ceremony within about twenty minutes. For most funerals that is perfectly adequate. If more time is required the undertaker must be told so that he can make the necessary arrangements. He should also be informed of any special requirements we may have such as the removal of religious symbols like crosses, and any special music we desire.

Music sometimes presents problems. At many places organists are provided who are perfectly competent, but most of them would be the first to admit that they are not first class musicians. There are also often music centres looked after by attendants who can be very possessive without necessarily being very competent. I once conducted a ceremony where the attendant created havoc. What made matters worse was the fact that the congregation was full of professional musicians, including sound engineers, but the attendant wouldn't let them near his precious equipment to sort things out.

Sometimes it is better to prepare your own music and use your own equipment provided the equipment is adequate for the size of the chapel. For most funerals all that is required is three or four minutes of music while people come in and about the same as people leave. If music is to be a special feature of the ceremony, the undertaker does need to know exactly what we wish to do.

This brings me to the actual shape and content of the ceremony. There are significant differences between a humanist and a religious ceremony.

A religious ceremony is an expression of religious faith. It focuses upon the god believed in and the promises made concerning life after death.

A humanist funeral is a celebration of the life that has been lived. It is an attempt to express simply and quietly our gratitude for a life we have shared and enjoyed. It is our way of bidding farewell with care, respect, and dignity. This means that no two humanist funerals are the same. We either work them out ourselves or we sit down with the celebrant and work things out together. There may be friends or relatives who wish to take part in the ceremony. There may be particular passages of literature or music which we wish to include. And there will normally be a tribute to the person who has died.

The tribute is usually the centre piece of the whole ceremony. The celebrant can pay our tribute provided we feed him or her with sufficient information, but this may come better from someone who actually knew our loved one.

When our loved ones die we are often left in a bit of a daze. But we do not need to worry. We can allow others to get on with coping until we are ready to take things back into our own hands again. The undertaker or funeral director is the first of these. So when your loved ones die, call the funeral director.

II. The Funeral Ceremony

With the passing of the centuries beliefs come and go, fashions and styles of mourning change. Customs vary from place to place. I don't know how things are today, but in the north of England women used to be excused attendance at the committal, and on the day of the funeral every curtain in the street would be drawn. At a burial every mourner would drop earth onto the coffin. In the south it was left to the sexton or the parson to drop earth on the coffin, women went to the whole funeral and neighbours didn't draw their curtains. Throughout the country widows wore black. Men raised their hats when a hearse passed. Now they don't even wear hats. Nor do many people feel the necessity to wear black, even at the funeral. Yet some feel strongly that they should.

At any funeral there are people holding a variety of different opinions. Some of us have a secular philosophy of life and are broadly humanist in our approach. We find this perfectly adequate in times of stress or grief. But there are others whose approach to life is religious. They believe that their religion can help them through such times.

It is important to be aware of our differences and sensitive to one another, but it is far more important to be aware of those universal human needs which bind us all together in the presence of death.

We need to find suitable ways in which to express our grief.

We need to honour those we have loved and to express our

love as generously as we can.

Sometimes it may be useful to look at the lives our loved ones have lived and to re-examine our own in the light of them, to ask whether we are living our lives the best way we can.

We also need to find the strength to begin our own lives again.

Since no two bereavements are the same and no two people are the same it follows that no two funerals should be the same. The shape of any funeral ceremony will depend a good deal on the level of family involvement.

Religious people often have the main ceremony in their own church and only go to a crematorium for the committal. Non-religious people occasionally have the main ceremony in their own home, a hall or a marquee, but it is far more usual to use the crematorium or the cemetery chapel for the whole thing.

Some *cemetery* chapels still leave a great deal to be desired. They are often cold and dingy with no provision for music. They were only provided for those second class citizens who could not afford or were refused a church ceremony and for those who hated the church so much that they wouldn't be seen dead with a parson.

Although things are different today, and crematoria are often very lovely places, the old cemetery chapels linger on and have not always been adequately upgraded. At a crematorium the main disciplining factor is the requirement that the ceremony be completed within twenty to thirty minutes. Within that timescale, as already mentioned, there is usually some music as people come into the building and also as they leave. For almost all funerals that is perfectly adequate. When we are stricken by grief the last thing we want is a ceremony that drags on and on interminably. Given those basics, the shape and content for the ceremony is entirely in the hands of the celebrant or the family. During the ceremony there will probably be a couple of buttons to press. The first will signal the time of committal. The family should be warned in advance that this can be a distressing moment. After all, this is the moment of final farewell. Sometimes the coffin disappears through a hatchway or down on a lift (rather like an old cinema organ); sometimes electrically operated curtains screen off the coffin from view. Some families prefer simply to leave the coffin on view until after they leave the chapel, thus avoiding any of these things.

The second button signals the end of the ceremony and tells the attendant and the undertaker's staff that it is time for them to open the doors and return to duty.

Within these constraints, what shape should the ceremony take? The simple answer is that it can take any shape at all.

Those of us who conduct humanist ceremonies will usually sit down with the families of those who have died to try to get a picture of what they want and of the mix of people who are likely to be present. Where clergy or ministers actually see people before a funeral they normally adopt a similar practice.

Some Christians regard a funeral as an evangelical opportunity when they can try to convert the non-Christian members of the congregation. That seems to me to be a very insensitive approach to people in distress.

We should aim to avoid giving offence. This will sometimes mean including elements in a funeral which are contrary to our own philosophy of life – but when we are swamped by grief we are not at our most logical.

Let me give two examples:

I once took the funeral of a Jew who was an atheist. Some members of his family were practising Jews. So they asked if they could conclude the ceremony with their standard prayer. At the appropriate time all the men whisked skull caps from their pockets, put them on, recited the prayer, and took them off again. To me it was thoroughly incongruous, but it mattered to them.

On another occasion I conducted the funeral of an atheist whose wife was what I can only describe as a superstitious Christian anxious about her insurance with her god. She was not a practising Christian but she did want to hedge her bets. So I conducted the funeral and then a clergyman saw to the committal (a burial). He attended my ceremony and obviously felt that it left something to be desired because his was the longest committal I have ever attended.

This kind of situation is comparatively rare but it is not uncommon for people to want a humanist ceremony and then to ask for a hymn or passage of scripture such as the 23rd psalm.

I don't think we should quibble about such things. When people are bereaved they should be given those things which help them at the time whether they fit in with our own ideas or not.

Sometimes people have so many ideas that the whole

ceremony takes shape in our conversation with them. More often, celebrants are left pretty much to their own devices. When I am left to my own devices I follow a similar pattern to that which is followed by most liturgical religious ceremonies. I do this for a number of reasons.

First of all, it is a kind of tribute to those who have prepared the religious ceremonies. A large number of people over many centuries have given their time, skill and care to providing something that will meet the needs of religious people within the constraints of time and so on that we have already mentioned. The content of their ceremonies will not be suitable for our use, but the style and the shape may well be useful.

It is useful first, because there are often religious people present at humanist ceremonies and we want them to feel reasonably at home.

It is useful second, because it helps undertakers and attendants at crematoria or at cemetery chapels to feel that they know where we are going. It helps build up a relationship of trust between these professionals and ourselves.

And the fact that the style and shape of a religious ceremony has proved satisfactory to many people may mean that something recognisably similar yet clearly different can prove satisfactory to the people we try to care for.

So I usually begin with a few sentences possibly taken from part two of this book. These are spoken as the coffin enters or immediately afterwards. My own practice is to join in the procession as a clergyman or minister would but it's not essential.

My normal order of ceremony would begin with a reading or two chosen by the family or taken from my own stock. Then I introduce the ceremony by speaking of the meaning of death in the context of this particular death and going on to speak of our desire to celebrate the life that has been lived.

Occasionally this will be followed by music and then any family contributions – usually readings and tributes – ending with my own tribute where that is desired.

For most of us the truly important people in the world are not those who hit the headlines but those to whom we are bound by the bonds of love and friendship, and especially the members of our own families. Their lives are part and parcel of our own so it is fitting that tributes should be as thorough and careful as possible.

After the tributes I normally have a period of quiet for personal reflection which gives those who have a religious philosophy of life an opportunity for prayer. This is often accompanied by music (I reckon that any piece of music within a funeral should rarely last much longer than three minutes because it can play such havoc with our emotions).

This leads on to the committal. From this point to the end of the ceremony it is wise to keep things fairly short. I normally follow a fairly set pattern and often include the familiar words 'earth to earth' (at a burial), 'dust to dust, ashes to ashes'. There is no necessity to do so but these words are so familiar that they tell everybody where we are in the ceremony and lead on to the dismissal which should be positive and forward looking. (Specimen funeral services are included in the booklet *Funerals Without God* by Jane Wynne Willson, published by the British Humanist Association.

Two forms of
Words for a Committal

The first is fairly traditional, derived from Marcus Aurelius, the Bible, Epicurus, Sophocles and Rupert Brooke:

> We came into the world with nothing and we were not afraid.
> We leave it with nothing. Let us go without fear.
> Death is part of the natural order of things.
> It belongs to the life of the world.
> It is the condition of our existence.
> It is no more than a simple dissolving of the elements
> whereof each living thing is composed . . .
> It is but nature's way so there is nothing to fear.
> So we commit your loved one to his/her natural end,
> (earth to earth)*, dust to dust, ashes to ashes, and
> celebrate the silent kiss that ends life short or long.
> (There shall be in that rich earth a richer dust concealed.)*

This second shorter form is an adaptation of words given me to read at the funeral of Kate Geraghty's mother:

We commit you
into the cycle of living and dying
(into the darkness and warmth of the earth)*
into the freedom of wind and of sunshine,
into the dance of the stars and the planets,
and into the richness and smiles of our memories.

*Words in brackets are usually only used for a burial.

III. Untimely Death

Some deaths are much harder to face than others. When those who die are young, grief may be hell.

We no longer face the fact of our mortality as early in life as we used to do. Back in the 1960s I lived in India for a while. At that time the average expectation of life was just over forty, and two out of three children died before they were five.

When life is that short you take your own mortality for granted. But when the average is up in the seventies, it is very easy to ignore the fact that none of us is guaranteed a tomorrow. After listening to a conversation between my father and one of his many grandchildren I wrote:

> When you grow up my grandson
> and schooldays are over for you,
> when all of your training is finished
> what do you think you will do?

> > I'm still very small my grandpa
> > like a bud on your favourite rose
> > and whether or not I shall flower
> > is something that nobody knows.

> > Make the most of the bud my grandpa,
> > take pleasure from what you can see.

> It's what I am now that matters,
> don't bother with what I will be.
>
> You are right my wise young grandson
> the bud is the thing to enjoy
> for my flower will be blown and over
> while you are no more than a boy.

I came to terms with my own mortality as a boy of seventeen. I was on holiday with my parents and my sister and we were walking near Land's End. I had lagged behind and was watching the sea crashing against the foot of the cliffs below.

In those circumstances water can have a dangerous attraction, a sort of drawing power. Perhaps this is what the ancient Greeks meant by the sirens. I have felt it often since – felt it with particular power inside a mountain in Switzerland watching the Trummelbach Falls.

On that day, watching the sea at Land's End, it came to me that (whatever it might mean to anybody else) it would not matter to me if I died there and then. I had had a good life; a complete life as far as it went.

From that moment I have known that *for the person who dies* it doesn't matter whether he/she is seven, seventeen or seventy. What matters is whether life has been good up to that moment.

If we have had a good life, death is meaningless to us. If we have not, death may well be that 'merciful release' so many people talk about.

It is only for other people, the loved ones we leave behind, that our death has meaning.

When I realised these things I knew that my own death would never worry me. I was ready for it whenever it came and I would live my life as fully as I could for as long as it lasted.

A long time ago I visited a teenage girl who was dying. She wasn't worried that she was dying – except for one thing. She was still a virgin and felt that she had missed out. Apart from that, though life had been brief it had been very good. Yet I still find myself thinking about her quite often – and she died over fifty years ago. If a friend's sense of loss continues, how much worse must it be for her family? The death of the young may not be a problem to those who die, but it is terrible for those who survive. And often grief is compounded by the circumstances of the death.

Cot death takes our babies; suicide our students; drug addiction and drink-driving take teens and twenties; crime kills; and 'aids' also attacks and destroys the young.

Although so very different, all these kinds of death pose special problems. However innocent we are, we often feel guilty. And it doesn't matter how reassuring other people are, we can still feel guilty. There is that awful 'if only. . .' hanging over us.

And we also feel that there are people who are pointing the finger of blame. I have had that finger of blame pointed at me and after forty years it still rankles and hurts.

When caring people lose a baby they are often inconsolable. None of us can watch over a child for twenty-four hours a day, but distraught parents constantly punish themselves for not being there at the crucial time. They are not blameworthy but they blame themselves nonetheless – and there are always those who will turn the screw.

All that anyone can do is to show faith in them and to support them with our ongoing love.

When older youngsters die, the responsibility is often clearer and sometimes all too clear. After a murder we blame the murderer. After a car crash we can often blame the folly or irresponsibility of car drivers. Sometimes in our search for relief from grief we damn too fiercely and our anger covers the fact that we do not feel entirely free from guilt ourselves.

It is very human and very understandable, but we should try to remember that the killers have their own burden of guilt to bear. Cursing them or punishing them may be necessary and helpful, but in the end we shall be left with our own grief and we shall have to find our own ways of coming to terms with it. We have lost someone we love. Hatred and bitterness will not bring that person back. It will only sour our own life and destroy it. Even if we cannot forgive, we must come to terms with what has happened and learn to live again.

One of the hardest deaths to face is that of a young suicide. I think particularly of one young student who actually came home to his loving, caring family at Christmastime and committed suicide at home. No family could have been more loving and supportive. Yet now they had to face the utter devastation of his

25

death and all the unanswerable questions it left behind. They are one of the loveliest families it has ever been my privilege to meet yet it happened to them.

Death from 'aids' also poses special problems. Whether the victim is heterosexual or not, families often feel ashamed and want no mention made of the cause of death. It is the Christian obsession with sex and with its own prurient morality which has created this shame and its attendant feelings of guilt. In this, as in so much else, religion is the source of much of humanity's pain instead of being a source of peace and healing.

Death from sexually transmitted diseases is not necessarily shameful at all. I have taken the funerals of many aids victims and have only rarely felt that there was any just cause of shame.

Where the victim is a homosexual or where a lesbian dies young there are often special problems of a kind rarely met in any other sort of death.

Families have often rejected their homosexual or lesbian children. Now that it is too late, they often want to ease their sense of guilt and their grief by making amends and they suddenly become very loving and possessive.

But their child has often become part of a new, gay or lesbian 'family'. Homosexuals and lesbians often form very loving, very supportive communities and these are as possessive and protective as the natal family that now suddenly appears on the scene.

A great deal of sensitivity and understanding is needed on all sides. In my experience, the gay/lesbian communities often show these qualities in a very marked degree.

Those of us who have to conduct the funerals of aids victims often feel that we are walking a tightrope. But it is a tightrope well worth walking. The rewards, if we can bring a measure of help and comfort all round, are enormous. I called this chapter 'Untimely Death' which is a daft heading when you come to think of it. Death is nearly always untimely. Usually it comes too early. But sometimes it comes too late. In that case our mourning often begins long before our loved one dies.

Accident, illness or advanced old age often mean that we see our nearest and dearest losing their faculties and becoming less than they once were. We grieve to see them thus, and we grieve and are angry because we are helpless to do anything for them.

26

Sometimes there comes a point where they are ready to die. The law still makes it impossible for anyone to help them on their way. We often feel angry with medical staff who feel as helpless as we do – although there are times when that anger is justified. There are times (usually for religious reasons) when doctors and nurses work too hard to keep people alive when life has become meaningless.

Joining a voluntary euthanasia society and/or writing a living will while we are still mentally competent may help to counter that particular problem.

But there are also occasions where, if we are honest, we have to admit that we wish our loved ones were dead because they are no longer the people we loved and respected. Hurt, shame, anger, guilt, grief, helplessness all combine to make us miserable and death often proves to be a genuine relief.

There are times when the real meaning of death is that those who survive can turn back to life. Colin Murray Parkes wrote: 'The essential message of a funeral is that in every ending there is a beginning.' That is also the essential message of death.

There is no greater honour we can pay to those whose lives are over than to turn back to life and to live it to the full. This does not imply forgetfulness or negligence or lack of respect. It simply means that we have learned (often from them) that 'life is for living'. They have had their lives. Part of ours still lies ahead.

But turning back to life is not always easy. Long term carers may have become isolated, imprisoned by the needs of the person to whom they have devoted so many years of their life. They may feel that it is very difficult to begin again, to take the first faltering steps back into a world that has moved on.

And if they are alone they may feel all the difficulty that is faced by those who are single or divorced. They are the odd one out, difficult to invite and shunned because it is felt to be awkward to converse with those who have recently faced death. They will need all the friendship and love we can give. That is it really. In this business of coping with death there are no experts and each death is unique. We have to find our own way through, picking up a crumb of help here and seeing a glimmer of light there.

Other people will usually not know how to help us, and if they are helpful it will often be by pure fluke. Except that they could not help at all but for the fact that they have shown their love and care and entered into our grief with that genuine sympathy which is the sharing of someone's experience.

Coping with death is the same as coping with life. It is simply a matter of drawing on the rich resources of our own humanity and taking strength from our own inner being. Beyond that, it is a matter of drawing on the reservoirs of friendship and love which we have built up over the years and with which we are surrounded.

I do not offer religion or mystique of any kind because I do not believe in them. We are just ordinary human beings, part of the natural world, living through nature's most dreadful storm and finding our way through to a peace of mind and spirit which is our own and all the better for that. With that peace comes the possibility of renewal of life – our very own life, to be lived in all its richness until it too comes to its end in death – a death which will be somebody else's problem.

IV. Life after Death?

Right through history there have been those who hankered after some sort of life after death and there have been those who did not. Our generation is no exception.

Within my own family, my mother had no interest in the subject and was completely agnostic about it. As far as she was concerned, she didn't know whether there was another life and she didn't care. That was the end of the matter.

My father, on the other hand, has been obsessed with the subject for as long as I can remember. His ideas involve a whole series of contradictions – but all of us are guilty of that from time to time. I suspect that he keeps them in separate watertight compartments and trots out whichever is pre-eminent at the moment. Sometimes he believes in a kind of afterlife school. We join the school at whatever level our life on earth has entitled us to and work our way up from say Class Three Heaven to Class Two and so on. At other times he believes in some form of human reincarnation. When I wrote this he was ninety-five years of age, so he was in no hurry to put his ideas to the test.

But enough of my family. Let us look a little wider.

In ancient times those who longed for life after death had fairly vague ideas and hopes. But they included using heavy stones to keep the dead down and prevent them from causing malicious harm to the living. They also included filling graves with the sort of possessions which might come in useful in another life: clothes, tools, weapons, wives, horses and servants.

As people tried to develop their thinking two kinds of idea became common: Hindus, Buddhists and others came up with some form of the reincarnation idea – the belief that we don't just live one life, we live a succession of lives. Sometimes this is seen as a progression towards the goal of absorption into the One, the All.

The other idea is more familiar to us in the West. It seems to have been developed first of all by a brotherhood of religious reformers in Palestine. They were known as the Hasidim and became the Pharisees of New Testament times.

It comes as something of a surprise to many people to learn that the Jews of Old Testament times had no real belief in life after death. Their ideas were not so very different from those of the Greeks. Hades or Sheol was the place of the dead. There the ghosts or shades lived on in a fairly meaningless kind of way. The dead Achilles told Odysseus that he would rather be a living slave than a dead prince.

The Hasidim developed the idea that after death there is a resurrection for those who have lived good or godly lives. A new life has been stored up for them with God.

Christians took this idea over and developed it, supporting it with miracles such as the raising of Lazarus from death by Jesus and the resurrection of Jesus himself. Moslems also took the idea over (initially from the Jews) and developed their own rather sensual idea of resurrection life.

There are many variants on the resurrection idea and I don't propose to examine them here. But I probably ought to mention that in addition to heaven for the saved, Christians also developed the idea of hell for the damned. Catholic Christians have two further ideas.

For people who have not been baptised into the Christian faith they provide a limbo which is very like the old ideas of Sheol or Hades. And for those Christians who are neither fit for heaven nor hell, they offer purgatory, an afterlife purification period rather like my father's afterlife school. Purgatory is a further preparation to enable people to enjoy heaven.

Nowadays only the more extreme kinds of Christian cling to the idea of damnation and hellfire.

In addition to belief involving reincarnation or resurrection there are spiritualist claims that it is sometimes possible to make contact with those who have died and to have limited converse with them. This is felt to be more likely in the early days after death. Although spiritualism has been attended by a great deal of hocus-pocus, there are some who hold their ideas with great sincerity. There is a similarity between these ideas and the primitive idea that as long as there is flesh on the bones the dead can come back to haunt us.

All of these ideas are based on hope rather than fact. They depend upon faith rather than evidence. For many the hope is winsome and the faith uncertain. For such people the value of their beliefs is slight. They may actually stand in the way of the discovery of the very real comforts we can derive from a purely human approach to bereavement.

But there are some religious people who hold their beliefs with passionate conviction and certainty. They are quite sure that they know the truth. That kind of certitude will obviously bring comfort to them. But when people with that kind of assurance try to impose their views on others, instead of providing comfort they often add to people's distress.

It is important to approach all these different ideas with sensitivity. After all, only a few would be arrogant enough to say categorically that there is no life after death. Without solid evidence we have to say that we do not know one way or the other. But we do emphasise that there is absolutely no solid evidence for any of these beliefs.

Humanists are not prepared to hold out a hope that may be false. And we are certainly not prepared to tell people to live their lives on the basis of a hope that may be false.

The absence of solid evidence suggests to us that this life is the only one we have; just as the absence of solid evidence suggests to us that there are no such things or persons as gods. So we live our lives on the assumption that this is the only one.

We do our best to make our lives as fulfilling and as satisfying as we can. Some people feel that this means that we have no comfort to offer to the bereaved. There are certainly some kinds of comfort which we cannot offer. But if those kinds of comfort are only based on hope or faith it is perhaps fair to ask whether anyone else ought to offer them either. We are certainly not prepared to offer a comfort that may turn out to be spurious. We are not prepared to offer an uncertain hope. But we have comfort to offer nevertheless. If I cannot make this clear in the next chapter, I'm quite sure that some of the passages that form the main substance of this book will do so for me.

V. Life after Bereavement

When people are overwhelmed by their grief it is hard for them to do anything more than grasp emotional comfort from those who are close to them. The best comfort just then is often to have someone sit with you and hold your hand; or to be held in the arms of someone who loves you.

But once the mind begins to function again, then all kinds of comfort can be found. We seek it within our own human situation. Because we do, it will never be quite the same twice because no two human situations are the same. There is often comfort to be found in the death itself. We speak sometimes of 'a merciful release'. And sometimes we can find comfort where none seems possible. I remember sitting with a young Irish girl, widowed after one month of marriage. Her husband had been a soldier. Early one morning he was driving to his barracks, skidded on black ice, and was killed in the crash. I sat with his widow, holding her hand and feeling absolutely useless. As we sat quietly together she said two things:

'Well at least he never killed anybody else in his life,' and 'I've been his wife. No one can ever take that away from me.'

She was beginning to use her mind to find her own comfort. In the end that is what we all have to do. Sometimes when we want to comfort bereaved people we wonder what we can possibly say that will help. But it is not so much what we say as what we hear that matters. Our primary task is to listen and to act as a sounding board. We enable people to express their grief and to get it out of their system – at least for the moment. We also help them to clutch at the first straws of comfort that come to their minds. If we are listening carefully enough, we can make the most of those straws.

And is that all?

Of course not. But it takes time to discover more lasting comfort.

It takes time to get the misery out of our system. And this is where an understanding friend can often be of immense help. Two or three weeks after the funeral the subject of the death in the family suddenly becomes tabu. No one refers to the person who has died because no one wants to open up old sores. And there we are bottling it all up with no one to talk to; no one to share what we are feeling. It is then that we need someone to come to us and make the first move:

'Do you want to talk about it?'

And it all pours out and it is such a relief. And we know that whenever we want to, here is a person who will listen as we talk about our loved one to our heart's content.

It also takes time to discover the comfort of memory. Nowadays adult families are often scattered all over the world so that we see each other rarely. Of course we can write letters. But most of us are bad correspondents. And we can telephone – but most of us have half a thought for the size of our telephone bill. Cheapest of all: we can think about our loved ones. In point of fact we can't avoid it. A thousand and one things will bring them to mind.

Exactly the same is true of those who have died. A thousand and one things bring them to our minds.

If we are part of a family we will often 'see' our loved ones again in gestures, expressions and ways of speaking and acting that have been passed on. And there are so many of the trivial things in life that bring our loved ones back to us vividly. Every time I put my foot on a chair to tie up my shoelace, I can hear my mother ticking my father off for the same crime.

What's more: memory doesn't fade. I was always told that it did. But my own experience is that the more you loved someone, the more their memory stays fresh and vivid. If that can be poignant it can also be joyful – and if you have let your loved one go, the poignancy fades but the joy continues.

All these kinds of comfort involve looking back and dwelling in the past. Is that all there is for us? Is there no life after bereavement? When we have lost our nearest and dearest is there any reason for us to go on living?

At first we may do little more than find comfort for today and a reason for tomorrow. But even that is enough to enable us to go on with life. The rest is partly a matter of time and partly a matter of will and determination.

Earlier in this chapter I mentioned the Irish girl who lost her husband. She was in her twenties when he died. It is obvious that someone in her position can start life again; create a new life; find a new love and build a new joy.

But what about those who are bereaved at the other end of life?

For me, it will always be my father who points the way. My mother died when they were both in their mid-eighties. They had celebrated their diamond wedding a year before she died. For the last few years of her life she had been crippled with arthritis and heavily dependent upon my father. She had been his life. When she died I expected him to follow.

Just how he summed up the will and energy to begin again I don't know. But he did. He began to do all those things he had told us that he wanted to do. I had never believed him. I thought that my mother was his excuse for not doing them. But I was wrong. He built a new life for himself to such purpose that people called him 'the happiest man in Rustington'.

It is true that he had many things going for him – supremely: health and energy. But I am convinced that more than anything else it was his attitude of mind that enabled him to triumph over his grief and begin again so successfully.

I used to visit an elderly woman who was completely housebound. But she retained her interest in her neighbourhood. She knew everything that was going on. When people visited she bombarded them with questions. Because she remained interested she remained interesting and alive. It was always a pleasure to visit her.

When the humanist is bereaved, have we nothing to offer? Of course we have.

There are the comforts the mind discovers in the midst of bereavement. There are the comforts provided by the surrounding circle of friends and loved ones. There are the ongoing comforts of joyful and amusing memories. There is the continuing life of our loved one in the lives of the rest of the family – the children and grandchildren – and in the things our loved one has done.

But the humanist whose mind is set so firmly on this world and this life, should also be able to turn without any lack of respect or feeling, firmly from the past. Lovingly we leave the past behind and set about the task of creating our own new future, however long or short that may be.

We sit down to dinner with my mother-in-law. When we have finished she is only half way through. How sad it would be if she failed to enjoy the rest of her meal just because we had finished. When our loved ones have completed their feast of life we can learn to go on to enjoy what is left of our own.

Note: My mother-in-law has died since these words were written – not quite as old as my father, she made 91!

VI. What about Anger and Guilt?

Some of the things I have written in this book have already had an airing in my magazine *The Humanist Theme*. Mrs. Vivien Gibson wrote to me when my articles appeared and said, 'What about anger? You have said nothing about anger.'

There must be many things connected with bereavement that I have left unmentioned – but she was right.

Many people do feel anger when they are faced with death and many people feel guilt.

Religious people are often so angry with their god for his injustice that they lose their faith. Others turn to religion in the hope that it can keep them close to the one who has died.

We are angry because life is so unjust. The young, the healthy, the 'good' are taken and those who long for death linger on indefinitely. So we are angry with life or with 'faith'.

We take it out on all sorts of people: doctors, nurses, social workers, caring relatives. Our anger makes us lash out in all directions. Often there is no justice in our anger and we know it, but we are angry just the same. And when we are angry we have to be angry with someone specific. Professionals are used to being attacked. That doesn't mean that they are not hurt when people are unjust, but they do understand. This is not always the case when we lash out at relatives and friends. We have carried a heavy load and we feel or say that they have failed to share it. Yet often, if we are able to be completely honest with ourselves, we shall find that they wanted to help but we were too possessive to allow them a chance to express their love.

If we could only escape from our preoccupation with ourselves we might discover that they are feeling guilty that they didn't do more. We often do feel that there are things we could have said or done and now it is too late. We regret so many lost opportunities and we feel ashamed that we didn't take more of them.

We are all imperfect. We all miss opportunities. We all have regrets.

But most of us did the best we could. We loved as best we could. Where we failed, our loved one understood and forgave us. After all, our loved one wasn't perfect either – almost, perhaps, but not quite.

Nothing in life is ever quite perfect. So we have to leave behind our past imperfections and get on with making the very best we can of the present and the future. If we have failed the loved one who has died, let us try to love those who are still alive that much more completely. It may be too late to reward those who have died, but if their death contributes to the well-being of the living we shall feel better about them.

Sometimes there are quite specific reasons for our anger or our guilt. When old people die it is usually easy to accept their death because they have had a good innings. It is the death of the young that really gets to us.

We are angry when war or famine, terrorism or disease takes our loved one. We are angry with politicians, terrorists, or a murderer or a driver because they have killed someone before time.

In the last few months I have taken the funerals of two cot death babies; a young man who drowned in his own vomit after an evening's drinking with friends; and two suicides. It could just as easily have been youngsters killed in road accidents or dying from drugs, aids or other illnesses.

Deaths of young people often make us angry at the sheer injustice of life. But they can affect us in much more personal ways. We may feel that we have in some way caused the death, or at very least failed to prevent it. So we are filled with remorse and are angry with ourselves and our closest companions. Or we may be angry with the person who has died. How dare he leave us? He had no right to go, leaving so many problems and burdens behind. He could still have been with us if only he had behaved differently. Or we are angry with his friends. And sometimes we feel guilty ourselves as if we drove him to his death.

It is perhaps this anger with ourselves and its associated feelings of guilt that is the hardest to bear. Why did we not do more, love better, express our devotion while we had the chance.

So many of us feel anger in the presence of death that it is clear that anger is a natural reaction to death.

I can't stress that enough: Anger is a natural reaction to death.

If we can recognise and accept that fact, we are half way to dealing with our own anger.

Anger needs to be both recognised and expressed. If we don't express it, it can easily turn into bitterness. Bitterness is no good to anyone. But if we express our anger we can get it out of our system and allow our minds to take over and make what sense they can of things.

Sometimes there isn't a lot of sense to be made. Life is often unjust and cruel. We have to learn to face that fact and to accept it with resignation. It has to be accepted, not because we approve of it, but because we can do nothing to alter it.

Where that is not the case; where we can do things to alter the injustice of life; grief and its attendant anger can often be the starting point of devoted work to improve the human lot. We all know of people who have suffered a death in the family (let us say from cancer or heart disease). Some of them go on to devote their time and resources to research into the causes and cure of that particular illness.

Under such circumstances our anger can lead to great benefit for other people and to the feeling that perhaps the suffering and death of our loved one were not altogether in vain.

So: if you feel angry, let your anger out. If it is possible feed it into appropriate channels that will turn it into something positive and good. And if that is not possible, at least get it out of your system and let your reason take over. Facing the death of a loved one is never easy. In the end the only real way to face it is to leave it behind. Our loved one has gone and we are left. Without disrespect, we must say our farewells and turn back to life. Time is short.

How short, none of us can know. Any loved one worth his salt will want his survivors to enjoy life to the full. The best way to cope with death is to turn back to life and live with all our power.

Postscript

I find that I have said very little about long term debilitating illnesses or about dementia. These are often the illnesses that make us most angry. And it is often our inability to cope with such illnesses that gives us much grief and leads us into feelings of guilt. Again and again I find myself faced with people who have done their utmost over a long period and their only reward is devastating internal turmoil and complete exhaustion.

There is no *quick* fix.

We need understanding, patient, loving friends or family. We need people who are equally ready to be with us or to stand back and allow us space. We probably need medical pick me ups and sleeping aids for a while. We need the chance to recover our strength and to build up our inner resources again – to recuperate.

When we have reached the bottom of the pit there is no further down that we can go. Then, if we search hard enough, we shall find that there are steps leading up out of the pit. And there are people above us who are holding out their hands to help us up.

Recovery and renewal *are* possible. New life *is* possible.

VII. Grief

Sometimes there is a bleak emptiness and desolation in grief. Tennyson captures it in one of his poems:

> 'Break, break, break,
> On thy cold gray stones, O sea!
> And I would that my tongue could utter
> The thoughts that arise in me.
>
> O well for the fisherman's boy,
> That he shouts with his sister at play!
> O well for the sailor lad,
> That he sings in his boat on the bay!
>
> And the stately ships go on
> To their haven under the hill;
> But O for the touch of a vanished hand
> And the sound of a voice that is still!
>
> Break, break, break,
> At the foot of thy crags, O Sea!
> But the tender grace of a day that is dead
> Will never come back to me.'

We have to find our own way past that and no one can do it for us. But when grief fills our whole being and seems so completely overwhelming and destructive we can see no way forward. Nor are we sure that we actually *want* to go forward and when people tell us that we must, we feel that they are being insensitive and cruel.

Yet these people are right. We can either go down Queen Victoria road and become the despair of our friends, self-pitying, self-destructive, withering and shrinking towards our own demise, or we can learn to grow and to live again.

No sensible person will ask us to deny our grief. What our friends will ask of us is that we *grow*, so that, instead of being all-embracing and all-encompassing, our grief becomes part of a larger whole.

People say all sorts of things about grief. They say that 'time heals' but that is not necessarily true. All that time does is to give us opportunities which we can take or reject. It gives us the opportunity to escape from the overwhelming nature of grief into something calmer, quieter and more positive just as a rushing river comes crashing into the quietness and stillness of a lake.

People also say that grief grows less with the years. Certainly the *pain* of grief may grow less. But if people are implying that we forget, then they are wrong. Where there has been real love and real loss, we never forget. Nor do we want to. On the contrary, we want to remember and to cherish what we have had. We want to carry our loved one with us into the future. But we have to learn to do that without allowing our grief to destroy our lives or to harm the lives of other people who love us. And sometimes that is not easy.

Have you ever tried to put something into a box only to find that it won't quite go? We try this way and that but it doesn't matter how many ways we try, it just won't fit. In the end we either break the box or behave more sensibly and go and find a larger box.

Our lives are within a box. For a while the box is so full of grief that there is no room for anything else. We have no intention of throwing the grief away. It is our connection with the life that has gone. What we need is a bigger box with room for our grief and also with room for all those new elements which can make the future bearable, possible, positive, even happy. So we have to grow the box – put in extra panels all round so that it becomes big enough to contain everything valuable from the past and everything we want to add in the future.

If we are really to work our way through our grief and come out of it the other side we have to learn how to be bigger, better and more complete people. That way we can take our loved ones with us and keep them safe in our hearts for the rest of our days but we can also start again and move on.

VIII. Returning to Joy

There are many different kinds of bereavement. All of them leave scars and all of them impose some kind of loneliness on us. For most of us the worst loneliness of all follows the death of a partner.

In countries like ours there are multitudes of lonely widows and widowers, all of them feeling that their experience is unique. There are times when all of us long for solitude but enforced solitude is a different matter altogether. Every little job becomes a burden. All the things we have always done and take in our stride suddenly seem mountainous. We long for someone to share the trivia of everyday life; for the companionship of an armchair filled.

Overcoming such loneliness is never easy. But it can be achieved. The very first thing we have to do is to learn not to be sorry for ourselves. Nothing loses friends so quickly.

Curiously enough, it is as we bully ourselves into doing those jobs we have been dreading that we begin to find the solace of an occupied body and mind. Whether we like it or not, life has to go on. As we begin to tackle the ordinary tasks of everyday life we find that our own death wish begins to fade. The normal human desire for life reasserts itself. It is time now to find and to focus on the joys of solitude.

As we have seen, memory is one of them. But memory is not unmitigated joy. Particularly in the early days it can bring as much desolation as comfort. It is only after what someone has called 'the healing years' that memory is all comfort.

Another of the joys of solitude is the rediscovery of ourselves. For years we have lived for someone else. Our lives have been governed at least in part, by our partner's wishes, our partner's way of life, pleasures, sensitivities, needs. Now we have only ourselves to consider. How do we want to spend our time? What do we want to do with ourselves and our lives?

There are new freedoms and new anxieties. I read once of a widow who had to conquer her fear of driving long distances alone. Most widows would first have to conquer the much more mundane fear of filling their own car with petrol. And widowers have to learn to cook, to clean and to shop.

In a way, it is going through a process of growing up all over again. We grow up into the new life that is ours. Every day we seem to face something new. But each day also brings a sense of accomplishment in what we have achieved. We begin to make all sorts of discoveries about ourselves and the vast untapped resources we possess.

Oddly enough, the supreme joy of solitude is the joy of companionship. Some areas of life close to us when we lose our partners. There are functions where everybody else is paired off and we feel out of place. But it often works the other way.

Precisely because we are alone, we are free to make new friends. We are freer to meet strangers, freer to talk and to listen. We no longer have to look over our shoulder wondering what our loved one would think of our friendship or our behaviour. We can respond freely and openly to every approach others make.

Solitude is often spoken about as a time of peace and tranquillity. Sometimes it may be. More often it is a time when our thoughts and feelings run riot and have to be brought under control. Someone called solitude 'a threshing floor of emotions'.

Provided we can separate grain and chaff we can turn our solitude into the secure base from which we venture out into our continuing journey through life. It is no insult to the memory of our loved ones to acknowledge that part of that adventure is only possible because they have gone. We travelled joyfully with them in the past. Now we are on a solo voyage which can also prove to be a lot of fun.

So smile through the tears, and when the tears are done smile on. There are joys still to come for those who will look for them and create them.

Part Two:

Comforting Words

Comforting Words

The rest of this booklet is given up entirely to passages which have brought comfort to people I have known.

As literature their quality may be very variable. But they all have their value and somewhere among them any reader should find something helpful.

Occasionally I add a comment of my own to show the way a particular passage has spoken to me or the thought it has provoked. I have also included a few of my own writings.

For many readers this part of the book will be the most useful of all. I hope that it will not only bring comfort but also stimulation so that readers will go on to seek out other passages which speak specifically and personally to themselves.

If it happens to be your task to conduct funerals, it may be that some of these passages may be useful within the framework of the ceremonies you create.

Note:
Since the first edition of this book there have been a large number of anthologies aimed at providing passages of comfort for people enduring grief and all sorts of material is now available on the internet too. As a result I have reduced and altered my anthology mostly to include material which is unlikely to be found easily elsewhere. I am grateful to all those authors who have given me permission to use their work.

Beannacht (Blessing)

On the day when
the weight deadens
on your shoulders
And you stumble,
may the clay dance
to balance you.

And when your eyes
freeze behind
the grey window
and the ghost of loss
gets in to you,
may a flock of colours,
indigo, red, green
and azure blue
come to awaken in you
a meadow of delight.

When the canvas frays
in the curach of thought
and a stain of ocean
blackens beneath you,
may there come across the waters
a path of yellow moonlight
to bring you safely home.

May the nourishment of the earth be yours,
may the clarity of light be yours,
may the fluency of the ocean be yours,
may the protection of the ancestors be yours.

And so may a slow
wind work these words
of love around you,
an invisible cloak
to mind your life.

c

After I Have Gone

Speak my name softly after I have gone.
I loved the quiet things, the flowers and the dew,
Field mice; birds homing; and the frost that shone
On nursery windows when my years were few;
And autumn mists subduing hill and plain
and blurring outlines of those older moods
that follow, after loss and grief and pain –
And last and best, a gentle laugh with friends,
All bitterness foregone, and evening near.
If we be kind and faithful when day ends,
We shall not meet that ragged starveling 'fear'
As one by one we take the unknown way –
Speak my name softly – there's no more to say –

But ah, 'tis sad, for us at least
who pass as vessels in the night,
and scarce can touch the hand to greet
ere fades the vision from our sight:

But I of you, and you of me
have given and taken lasting things:
the silent, mystic, subtle power
which mind on mind forever flings.

There would be no shadows
if the sun were not shining.

(Carried by the late Stan Burton in his wallet.)

Come not with Tears

Come not with tears to where I lie,
When all my days and years go by.
   Say that you ever hold me dear
     and I shall hear.

Lay no red roses on the spot
But lilies and forget-me-not.
   And if you say "I miss you so"
     my heart will know.

Mourn not for me, but passing there,
Speak, in your heart, a silent prayer.
   Say that my love your life has blest
     and I shall rest.

I expect to pass through
this world but once:

any good thing therefore
that I can do, or any
kindness that I can show
to any fellow creature,
let me do it now;

let me not defer or
neglect it, for I shall not pass this
way again.

A.D.1420

I do not seek to live for millions of years beyond this life, whether in a state of infinite bliss or otherwise. Nor do I have any expectation that I or any other creature will ever do so.

The very fact of having lived, for however brief a time, is a fact of ineradicable immortality. The babe that lives only for a day, indeed, even the foetus that is miscarried or aborted, is not without some permanent and enduring effect by having some impact, however insignificant, on the minds and actions of those who are aware of it.

There is no absolute death while any memory remains with those continuing to live. Where genes too have been passed on, the consequences will represent true and everlasting immortality. This is an inescapable and demonstrable fact.

All those we have ever known live on in us in varying degrees, with ever changing force and vividness, and we live on in all others who have known us or taken genes from us. Mere forgetfulness makes no difference.

(To my shame I don't remember the name of the gentleman in Wimbledon who wrote this in preparation for his own funeral.)

J'ai écrit ton nom sur le sable
    mais la vague l'a effacé.
J'ai gravé ton nom sur un arbre
    mais l'écorce est tombee.
J'ai incrusté ton nom dans le marbre
    mais la pierre a cassé.
Alors j'ai enfoui ton nom dans mon coeur
    et le temps l'a gardé.

I wrote your name on the sand
    but the wave washed it away;
I carved your name on a tree
    but the bark has fallen;
I inlayed your name in marble
    but the stone has broken;
I buried your name in my heart
    and time has preserved it.

After Glow

I'd like the memory of me
to be a happy one.
I'd like to leave an after glow
of smiles when life is done.
I'd like to leave an echo
whispering softly down the ways,
Of happy times and laughing times
and bright and sunny days.
I'd like the tears of those who grieve,
to dry before the sun
of happy memories
that I leave when life is done.

Look for me when the tide is high
And the gulls are reeling overhead
When autumn wind sweeps the cloudy sky
And one by one the leaves are shed.

Look for me when the trees are bare
And the stars are bright in the frosty sky
When the morning mists hang in the air
And shorter darker days pass by.

I am there when the river flows
And salmon leap to a silver moon
Where the insects hum and tall grass grows
And sunlight warms the afternoon.

I am there in the busy street
I take your hand in the City Square
In the market place where the people meet
In your quiet room I am there.

I am in the love you cannot see
And all I ask is you look for me.

———————————

'Now we are old we know that we must die;
Our spirits will be one with earth and sky;
Should you go first, I know that I shall find
That though you're gone, your love has stayed behind.'

———————————

I had thought that your death was a waste and a destruction . . . I
am beginning to learn that your life was a gift and a growing . . .
The fact of death cannot destroy what has been given. I am
learning to look at your life again instead of your death and your
departing.

It seems to me that the life of man on earth is like the swift flight of a single sparrow through the banqueting hall where you are sitting at dinner on a winter's day with your captains and counsellors. In the midst there is a comforting fire to warm the hall. Outside, the storms of winter rain and snow are raging. This sparrow flies swiftly in through one window of the hall and out through another. While he is inside, the bird is safe from the winter storms, but after a few moments of comfort, he vanishes from sight into the wintry world from which he came. So, man appears on earth for a little while but what went before this life, or of what follows, we know nothing.

A seventh century Northumbrian.

Ask Me

Not how did he die, but how did he live?
Not, what did he gain, but what did he give?
These are the units to measure the worth
Of a man as a man, regardless of birth
Not what was his church, not what was his creed
But had he befriended those really in need?
Was he ever ready, with the word of good cheer,
To bring back a smile, to banish your tears?

Sometime at eve when the tide is low
I shall slip my mooring and sail away
With no response to the friendly hail
Of kindred craft in the busy bay.

In the silent hush of the twilight pale
When the night stoops down to embrace the day
And the voices call in the water's flow . . .
Sometime at eve when the tide is low
I shall slip my mooring and sail away.

Through the purpling shadows that darkly trail
O'er the ebbing tide of the Unknown Sea
I shall fare me away, with a dip of sail
And ripple of waters to tell the tale
Of a lonely voyager, sailing away
To the Mystic Isles where at anchor lay
The craft of those who have sailed before
O'er the Unknown Sea to the Unseen Shore.

A few who have watched me sail away
Will miss my craft from the busy bay
Some friendly barques that were anchored near,
Some loving souls that my heart held dear,
In silent sorrow will drop a tear –

But I shall have peacefully furled my sail
In moorings sheltered from storm or gale
And greeted the friends who have sailed before
O'er the Unknown Sea to the Unseen Shore

When I am dead,
Cry for me a little,
Think of me sometimes
But not too much.

Think of me now and again
As I was in life at some moment
That is pleasant to recall
but not too long.

Leave me in peace
And I shall leave you in peace.
And whilst you live
Let your thoughts be with the living.

When I am Gone

When I am gone,
release me, let me go,
You mustn't tie yourself to me in tears.
Be happy that we had so many years.

I gave to you my love,
You can only guess
how much you gave to me
in happiness.

Grieve awhile for me
if grieve you must,
then let your grief be comforted.
I trust

you'll bless the memories
that I have sown
and I thank you
for the love you each have shown.

(I have revised this anonymous piece.)

When I must: leave you for a little while
Please do not grieve and shed wild tears
but hug your sorrow to you through the years.
But start out bravely with a gallant smile
And for my sake and in my name
Live on and do all things the same
Feed not your loneliness on empty days
But fill each working hour in useful ways.
Reach out your hand in comfort and in cheer,
And I in turn will comfort you and hold you near.

(Left by Jack Burrows for his wife Siggy.)

You're not alone as the seasons change. . .

As you continue life's journey on your own,
remember you are not alone.
Although that familiar voice
can no longer be heard,
there is a living presence in everyday things . . .

in the snowflakes that fall on a cold winter's night,
in the morning chorus of singing birds in spring,
in the touch of a warm summer's breeze,
and the gentle float of autumn leaves,
there is a living presence in everyday things . . .

Here lies a poor woman who was always tired.
She lived in a house where help wasn't hired.
Her last words on earth were: Dear friends, I am going
To where there's no cooking, or washing, or sewing.
For everything there is exact to my wishes.
For where they don't eat there's no washing of dishes.
I'll be where loud anthems will always be ringing.
But having no voice I'll be quit of the singing.
Don't mourn for me now, don't mourn me never.
I am going to do nothing for ever and ever.

They say there is a reason.
They say that time will heal,
but neither time nor reason
will change the way I feel.
For no one knows the heartache
That lies behind our smiles,
No one knows how many times
We've bent our heads and cried.

We want to tell you something, so
there won't he any doubt.
You're so wonderful to think of
and so hard to live without.

We don't have to be religious to share these sentiments from a prayer of Francis of Assisi:

Where there is hatred, let us sow love;
where there is injury, pardon;
where there is discord, union;
where there is despair, hope;
where there is darkness, light;
where there is sadness, joy.

May we not so much seek
to be consoled as to console,
to be understood as to understand,
to be loved as to love;
for it is in giving that we receive,
it is in pardoning that we are pardoned.

I have met many of the following authors, through conducting funerals for them:

The Loss of a Dad
(written for Victor Brock by 'Sue'.)

The days seem cold and lonely,
the skies seem bleak and sad,
the sun just isn't shining
now we have lost our dad.

There's going to be an empty space
which no one else can fill
for nobody can take his place
and no one ever will

and all the words of sympathy
which friends and family send
are not enough to heal our pain
or make our sadness end.

The love we shared was special
and the things we did together
are safely stored inside our hearts
and they'll be there for ever.

A Verse

The tide recedes but leaves behind
   bright seashells on the sand.
The sun goes down and gentle warmth
   still lingers on the land.
The music stops and yet it echoes on . . .
   in sweet refrain.
For every joy that passes
   something beautiful remains.

M.D. Hughes

Snuffing Zone

Somewhere there is a driver
who killed our cat. Upset,
at what had happened, ignorant
of which house in a London street
was hers, they laid her reverently
two doors from home.

'Shall I let her out?' I'd asked.
'As you wish,' you said.
I found her stiff, unmarked,
a little blood and liquid on the stone,
caught leaping, tail outstretched
like the tiger in the ad.

Burying her in the territory
she'd ruled for two decades
we found a paving stone
we'd never known of,
as if in death
she'd led us to new mystery.

Somewhere there is a driver
who saved our cat from death
by failing kidneys.
Now that I am entering the snuffing zone,
may I be let out on a warm night,
caught on the prowl for gossip, sex or power
and laid out reverently
and, dying, reveal another mystery.

Anthony Barnes

Translation of
The Discourse on Loving-Kindness

If you are wise and want to reach the state of peace,
you should behave like this:
You should be upright, responsible, gentle and humble.
You should be easily contented and need only a few things.
You should not always be busy.
You should have the right sort of work.
Your senses should be controlled and you should be modest.
You should not be exclusively attached to only a few people.
You should not do the slightest thing
that a wise person could blame you for.
You should always be thinking: May all beings be happy.
Whatever living beings there are, be they weak or strong,
big or small, large or slender, living nearby or far away,
those who have already been born
and those who have yet to be born,
May all beings without exception be happy.
You should not tell lies to each other.
Do not think that anyone anywhere is of no value.
Do not wish harm to anyone, not even when you are angry.
Just as a mother would protect
her only child at the risk of her own life,
So you should let the warmth of your heart go out to all beings.
Let your thoughts of love go through the whole world
with no ill-will and no hate.
Whether you are standing, walking, sitting or lying down,
So long as you are awake you should develop this mindfulness.
This, they say, is the noblest way to live.
And if you do not fall into bad ways,
but live well and develop insight,
And are no longer attached to all the desires of the senses,
Then truly you will never need to be reborn in this world again.

from Buddhism

Good wishes
(Celtic/American Indian?)

When you are lonely, I wish you love.
When you are down, I wish you joy,
When you are troubled, I wish you peace,
When things are complicated,
                    I wish you simple beauty,
When things are chaotic,
                    I wish you inner silence,
When things look empty, I wish you hope.

_____

Don't cry for me but be glad
and remember all the good times we've had,
For when I go through death's dark door
I shall be happy with those who have gone before.
And if there's nothing – no heaven, no hell,
then I shall be nothing with them as well.
And you don't cry for nothing, that's a waste of tears
so don't cry for me – my dears!

Kay Chalke

_____

Don't think of me at all – if you think of me with tears
But remember me with laughter if you think of me my dears!

Kay Chalke

For Mum

Now that you're free
I'll embrace you in the wind.
Feel you in the rain
And see you in the stars.

Now you're free
I'll have you in my thoughts,
Hold you in my heart,
Sing you in my songs.

I will never walk alone,
Never lose your love, nor will you mine.
Now you're free
I will have you through my life,
I will know you for all time.

**by Chris for his mother,
Barbara Dunwoodie**

Death

Death is to be wrapped in the dreamless
drapery of eternal peace . . . Upon the
shadowy shore of death the sea of trouble
casts no wave. Eyes that have been
curtained by the everlasting dark will
never know again the burning touch of tears.
Lips touched by eternal silence will never
know what it is to speak the broken words
of grief.

R.C. Ingersoll

The Parting Glass – a traditional song
adapted by Sarah Matthews and me.

Oh all the time that e'er I've spent
   I spent it in good company.
And of all the love that e'er I shared
   I shared with you so easily.
And all I've done from want of wit
From memory now I can't recall
   So fill to me the parting glass:
Goodnight, and joy be with you all.

Oh all the days that e'er I've toiled
   I gave them up so willingly.
And all the ones that e'er I've taught
   Will carry on my legacy.
And all the bonds in family made
With warmth and pleasure still remain
   So raise your glass and drink a toast:
Goodnight, and joy be with you all.

Oh all the friends that e'er I've made
   Are sorry for my going away
And all the family I've had
   Would wish me one more day to stay
But since it falls unto my lot
That I should part and you should not
   I'll gently part and softly call:
Goodnight, and joy be with you all.

Your day has come, no more tomorrows,
You are free at last of all your sorrows,

The rain has fallen and washed away your pain,
The sun has shone and you smile again.

Let us look up into the sky,
Your wings are waiting to take you high,

We hear your laughter as you start to fly,
When we hear the wind we will know you're near by.

Farewell for now, until we meet again,
With eternal love for you: Good bye.

by Sharon Newman for her father
(when she was 15 years old)

An Ancient Sanscrit Poem

Look to this day for it is life,
the very life of life.
In its brief course lie all
the realities and truths of existence,
the joy of growth,
the splendour of action,
the glory of power.

For yesterday is but a memory
and tomorrow is only a vision.
But today well lived
makes every yesterday a memory of happiness
and every tomorrow a vision of hope.
Look well, therefore, to this day.

The Time that we Spent Together

Don't say I'm leaving,
I'm just moving on.
Such a very small change,
different key for my song.
Back here for tea
you won't notice I've gone.

I looked for a job
but it's so hard to find one.
I looked for a man,
just a quiet and kind one.
Then I looked through the window,
looked up at the sky,
looked into their faces as people passed by,
I saw every expression that's under the sun:

do you think that it's true
that we are what we've done?

It's Possible to End Happily

It's possible to end happily,
possible to end happily
without saying prayers or winning battles,
without being obsessed with goods and chattels.

It's possible to end happily,
possible to end happily
without low cunning or high position,
without self interest or grand ambition,

but you do need a friend
or two or four,
or six or eight
or ten or more . . .

*from poems written by Neil O'Malley
and used at his funeral.*

Life's Kite

Wind buffeted, life's kite
(umbilical cord which I held tight)
was soaring in the yellow light.

Pulling me with all its might
and reaching for the heavenly height
it soars away on lonely flight.

It was very nearly lost to sight
when it broke free. The loss was slight
for through my pain I felt it right.

**(a poem by Charlie Garnell
which I have re-written)**

From a code of Canadian Indians

Treat the earth and all that dwell thereon with respect.
Show great respect for your fellow beings.
Work together for the benefit of all mankind.
Give assistance and kindness wherever needed.
Do what you know to be right.
Look after the well-being of mind and body.
Dedicate a share of your wealth to the greater good.
Be faithful and honest at all times.
Take full responsibility for your actions.

Live Your Life

Live your life that the fear of death
can never enter your heart.
Trouble no one about his religion.
Respect others in their views
and demand that they respect yours.
Love your life, perfect your life,
beautify all things in your life.
Seek to make your life long
and of service to your people.
Prepare a noble death song for the day
when you go over the great divide.
Always give a word or sign of salute when meeting
or passing a friend, or even a stranger, if in a lonely place.
Show respect to all people but grovel to none.
When you rise in the morning, give thanks for the light,
for your life, for your strength.
Give thanks for your food and for the joy of living.
If you see no reason to give thanks,
the fault lies in yourself.
Touch not the poisonous firewater that makes
                                  wise ones turn to fools
and robs the spirit of its vision.
When your time comes to die, be not like those
whose hearts are filled with fear of death,
so that when their time comes they weep and pray
for a little more time to live their lives over again
in a different way.
Sing your death song, and die like a hero going home.

Chief Tecumseh of the Shawnee Nation (1768-1813)

From the Letters of Seneca

There's nothing to stop you enjoying the
company of absent friends, as often as you
like to, and for as long as you like . . .

Everyone of us is absent to a great extent
from his friends even when they are around.
Count up the times spent apart from one another . . .

Thinking of departed friends is to me
something sweet and mellow. For when I
had them with me it was with the feeling
that I was going to lose them, and now
that I have lost them I keep the feeling
that I have them with me still . . .

Possession of a friend should be in the
mind: the mind's never absent: it
sees daily whoever it likes. Life would
be restricted indeed if there
were any barrier to our imaginations.

I see you my friend . . . I hear you at
this very moment. I feel so very much
with you.

Attributed to Robert Louis Stevenson:

He has achieved success who has lived well,
laughed often and loved much;
who has gained the respect of other people
and the love of little children;
Who has found his own niche
and accomplished his tasks;
who has worked to make his own world
better than he found it;
who has looked for the best in others
and given the best he had;
Whose life was an inspiration;
Whose memory is a benediction.

Five verses from *Daphnaida* – an Elegy
by Edmund Spenser (1552 – 1599)

She fell away in her first ages spring,
Whil'st yet her leafe was greene, and fresh her rinde,
And whil'st her braunch faire blossomes forth did bring,
She fell away against all course of kinde,
For age to dye is right, but youth is wrong;
She fell away like fruit blowne down with winde,
Weepe, Shepheard! weepe, to make my undersong.

Yet fell she not as one enforst to dye,
Ne dyde with dread and grudging discontent,
But as one toyld with travaile downe doth lie,
So lay she downe, as if to sleepe she went,
And closde her eyes with carelesse quietnesse;
The whiles soft death away her spirit hent,
And soule assoyld from sinful fleshlinesse.

I will walke this wandring pilgrimage,
Throughout the world from one to other end,
And in affliction wast my better age;
My bread shall be the anguish of my mind,
My drink the teares which fro mine eyes do raine,
My bed the ground that hardest I may find;
So will I wilfully increase my paine.

Ne sleepe (the harbenger of wearie wights)
Shall ever lodge upon mine ey-lids more;
Ne shall with rest refresh my fainting sprights,
Nor failing force to former strength restore;
But I will wake and sorrow all the night
With Philomene*, my fortune to deplore;
With Philomene, the partner of my plight.

And ever as I see the starres to fall,
And underground to go to give them light
Which dwell in darkness, I to minde will call
How my fair Starre (that shinde on me so bright)
Fell sodainly and faded under ground;
Since whose departure, day is turned to night,
And night without a Venus starre is found.

*Philomene = the nightingale.

In the midst of life we are in death

Life comes and goes.
The existence of man fluctuates,
tragic situations bring out the best in people,
love and understanding bind the broken-hearted.

The death of a friend so young
makes us reject
the averages of life,
and some of the world's values.

Life may be long
or short.
We must make the most of what we have,
live life to the full.

And we must come to terms with death,
not grieve excessively.
Time cannot cure the intense heartache
but may ease the pain.

Christine Scrase

(One of her early poems which I have adapted slightly.)

I Wish

from a poem by Mark Shuckburgh written
for his brother-in-law Richard Stokes - 7.12.1998

I wish your days would never end.
I wish you were still with us now.
I wish your days would never end.
Our love is in full flow.

Those memories of how you were
will fill our waking hours.
Those memories of how you were,
we'll hold them tight. They're ours.

They'll never, ever come again,
those days of you and me
but all the memories remain
of all you used to be.

d

A few Favourite Sentences and Verses:

We live in deeds, not years;
In thoughts, not breaths;
In feelings,
not in figures on a dial.
Philip James Bailey

Away with funeral music,
Set the pipes to powerful lips:
The Cup of Life is for him who drinks it,
and not for him who sips
Robbie Burns

O Death, the poor man's dearest friend,
The kindest and the best.
Robbie Burns
(I sometimes substitute 'sick' for 'poor'.)

Because I have loved life,
I shall have no sorrow to die.
Amelia Josephine Burr

And when life needs no more of us at all,
Love's word will be the last that we recall.
John Drinkwater

O tranquil peace so long desired,
we sense the night's soft breath.
How tired we are of travelling.
Can this perhaps be death?
Joseph von Eichendorf

If I had strength enough to hold a pen,
I would write how easy and pleasant a thing it is to die.
John Hunter, Surgeon, *on his death bed (1793).*

If so much that is precious can so soon be lost,
let me cherish what remains;
and let me be the nurture
of things precious in the lives of others.
Quoted in *The Inquirer* by **K.G.**

In the circle of friends, the one who dies first
is the friend you will never forget;
this is the death that unhinges you . . .
Alice Kavounas

And, as she looked around, she saw how death, the consoler,
Laying his hand upon many a heart, had healed it for ever.
Longfellow

Rest assured therefore that we have nothing to fear in death. Once
this mortal life has been usurped by death there can be no more
suffering . . . If the life we have lived till now has been a pleasant
thing, we can retire as a guest who has had his fill of life and take
our carefree rest with a quiet mind
Lucretius

Make use of life while you have it.
Whether you have lived long enough depends upon yourself,
not on the number of your years.
Montaigne

If there's another world, he lives in bliss;
If there is none, he made the best of this.
Epitaph on the grave of **William Muir**

A man lives for as long as we carry him inside us,
For as long as we carry the harvest of his dreams,
For as long as we ourselves live
Holding memories in common, a man lives.
Brian Patten *from* **Pablo Neruda**

This is good fortune, to end our lives with honour . . .
One's sense of honour is the only thing that does not
grow old, and the last pleasure, when we are worn out
with age is . . . having the respect of our fellows.
Pericles (acc. to Thucydides!)

No more a tired heart downcast or overcast,
No more pangs that wring or shifting fears that hover,
Sleeping at last in a dreamless sleep locked fast.
Christina Rossetti

Death may appear more friendly
and come more gently when we are old,
just as the softness of dusk
precedes the darkness of night.
>> *Dr. Joan Simkins*

Glad did I live and gladly die
And I laid me down with a will.
>> *Robert Louis Stevenson*

Death is the final and greatest healing of all,
as we leave illness and all the other trials and
tribulations of this life behind.
>> *Frank Williams*

And when the stream that overflows has passed,
A consciousness remains upon the silent shore of memory;
Images and precious thoughts that shall not be
and cannot be destroyed.
>> *William Wordsworth*

What though the radiance which was once so bright
Be now for ever taken from my sight,
Though nothing can bring back the hour
Of splendour in the grass, of glory in the flower:
We will grieve not, rather find
Strength in what remains behind . . .
>> *William Wordsworth*

The thought of death sits easy on the man
who lives close to the countryside . . .
We have no need of names and epitaphs;
we talk about the dead by our fire-sides . . .
In each other's thoughts
we each possess a kind of second life . . .
>> *William Wordsworth*

O Friend . . . Far art thou wandered now . . .
But thou art with us, with us in the past,
The present, with us in the days to come,
There is no grief, no sorrow, no despair,
No languor, no dejection, no dismay,
No absence scarcely can there be, for those
Who love as we do.
                    William Wordsworth

The important thing about our lives
is not how or where they end
but the people they touch
and the things they achieve on the journey.

Let us mourn our loved ones, not with lamentations,
but by keeping their memory fresh in our hearts.

I know that the day will come
when my sight of this earth shall be lost
and life will take its leave in silence
drawing the last curtain over my eyes.

Yet stars will watch at night
and morning rise as before.

When I give up the helm
I know that the time has come
for others to take it.

What there is still to do will be done.
I have no need to struggle on.

Some of the author's own pieces:

Going to a funeral

Going to a funeral is a bit like going
to a railway station to say goodbye to
someone we love. As the train moves
slowly away from us we wave goodbye and
watch them out of sight until the last
trace of the train is gone.

Sometimes, of course, we are reasonably
cheerful because we know that it will
not be long before we stand waiting for
their train to arrive.

But as we grow older we are less sure.
Will this be the final farewell? Their
train moves away and we feel that we may
never enjoy another arrival. We leave
the station with sadness in our hearts
as we turn back to the continuation of
our own lives.

So it is with death. We see the departure
and know that there is no return. But after
a while we begin to realise that we can
never lose those things we already have.
We can never lose the experiences of love
that we have shared nor can we ever lose
the rich fund of memories that our shared
lives have given to us.

*While reading Tennyson's **Idylls of the King***

I would not be holy
as the hermit or the monk.

No. I would come to death
from the heart of the world's life
bearing the scars of many battles.

And some will be the scars of victory,
and some, borne sad but openly,
the marks of my defeat.

The good fight I would fight,
though fight and often lose,
and thus would come through life.

Let me but reach my end
open and honest
and without hypocrisy.

Death

When I was a boy
I sometimes went to bed
by candlelight.

The last task
was to blow out the candle
or snuff it out
between finger and thumb.

Death is no more than that –
a negative,
it is not man's enemy.

In simple truth
it is precisely that,
nothing at all,
just the snuffing out of life's flame.

. . . to Quietness and Sleep

In the night of weariness
I will not force my flagging spirit
nor drive my overburdened mind,
nor yet persist
with pointless fears
or vain imaginings.

Night draws its veil
over the tired eyes of the day.
I leave behind the confusion,
the noise and clamour of my life's concerns
and give myself up
to quietness and sleep.

Perhaps to sleep for ever,
but whether for me or for you
the darkness will vanish
and the morning will surely come
to renew the sight with dawn
in a fresh gladness of awakening.

(This owes much to the poems of Rabindranath Tagore.)

Life's Pool

We are like children
with hands full of stones
standing beside a pool of still water.

One by one we cast the stones
filling the pool with ripples
counteracting one another
or blending with one another.

But the ripples die away.

The pool returns to stillness
when the last stone
has been thrown.

On the Death of a Child

and when she died
we mourned our loss
and cried in anger
and in pain.

we soldiered on
took strength from friends
who wrapped us round
and took the strain.

between ourselves we shared our love
and shared our pain,
we found our way
to life again.

we're stronger now
live deeper lives,
and all because
she came and died.

Death

The struggle of life is ended
in silence and in sleep.

Oblivion comes
and rest from pain
and peace from care.

No more the haunted soul,
no more the tortured mind,
no more the fevered brow.

Oblivion comes
and rest from pain
and peace from care.

A hymn: Life's Full Circle

Life has many things to offer,
love brings joy beyond compare;
not in solitude we find them,
family and friends all share.

Excellence is what we strive for,
wholeness is the human goal.
So we seek our own fulfilment
in a caring, sharing role.

Eagerly we grasp life's riches,
eagerly we set them free,
prodigal with what life gives us,
glad a source of joy to be.

And in times of pain and crisis
or in sorrow's lonely hour
we bring home the strength and solace
of our love's renewing power.

Swift our lives run their full circle
'from the cradle to the grave',
so we live each day's adventure
to the full, and nothing save.

Then, when falls life's final curtain,
peacefully we take our rest
leaving those who love and mourn us
knowing that we lived our best.

This may be sung to the tune specially written for it: *Life's Full Circle* by Brendon Renwick, or to the hymn tune: *Love Divine*.

Death Wishes

Dear medics,
       there's no need to strive
so hard to keep this chap alive.

I've had far more of weal than woe
and if it's now my time to go
I'm pretty nearly umpty five
and unconcerned if death arrive.

Use all the bits of me you can
to help some other maid or man.

Those who survive me will agree
tis better to go with dignity
than cling to some poor hollow sham
an ancient relic of a man.

If I were conscious or au fait
I'd end things now and not delay.

I've no religion and no god
so, even if you think it's odd,
I pray you let me go in peace –
as far as may be from a priest.

Grief

Death may be nothing
but grief is hell.
The agony of loss
and no one to tell.

The plans destroyed,
the emptiness of life;
the things unsaid
to husband or wife.

'Ashes to ashes and
dust back to dust',
and the long slow journey
back to life if I must.

Life's Joys

Thankful am I that I have lived in this great world
And known its many joys:

the thrill of mountains
and the morning air,
hills and the lonely heather covered moors,
harvest and the strong sweet scent of hay;

a rock-strewn river overhung with trees,
shafts of sunlight in a valley leading to the sea,
the beat of waves on rough and rocky shores
and wild, white spray flung high in ecstasy:

the song of birds awakening at dawn
and flaming sunsets at the close of day
with cooling breezes in the secret night –
music at night and moonlight on the sea;

the comfort of my home and treasured things,
the love of kin and fellowship of friends,
firelight and laughter and children at their play
with all their hopes and dreams,
their freshness as the future beckons them;

the faithful eyes of dogs, companionship of cats,
my garden with its rich reward for toil,
and all those things that make life dear and beautiful.

The tapestry of life, both joy and pain
is ours to live but once and not again.
When I look back upon my richly varied years,
I crave no more.
Thankful am I that I have lived
So shed no tears.

(This began as somebody's prayer. I have re-written it so many times that I have no idea how much of the original remains and must apologise to the unknown original author.)

A Grave

It's good to have a place to go,
a place of pilgrimage you know,
a place to pause, remember, think and stare,
a place to feel that he is there.

It's good to have a place to go
where we can say, 'we miss you so'.
In this calm spot we are at ease
knowing that you have found your peace.

We know we must begin again
and find new ways to ease our pain
but there will always be a space
within our hearts – your own dear place.

And sometimes as we slip away
we'll almost seem to hear you say,
'Thanks for the past. It meant so much.
Through heart and mind you'll keep in touch.'

Nothing from the Past has Gone

When someone dies,
someone from our family
or a close and well-loved friend,
somehow we feel
that we are less than once we were.

Reduced in stature,
something in ourselves has died,
something of our life has gone,
irretrievably gone
and lost for ever.

Slowly, so slowly, we discover deeper truths.
Nothing has gone save only the present and future presence,
the warm companionship
that has meant so much.

All that we have ever known remains:
all the memories we have treasured,
all the fun and all the laughter,
all the love and all the friendship:
nothing from the past has gone.

(After reading John Donne's famous poem.)

'Ad gloriam per spinas'

Life is not always kind or good.
Sometimes it seems
that fate has dealt
a rotten hand.

Each rising tide
is followed by the ebb.
Each minor victory
is beaten down.

And yet folk battle on,
grim-faced, determined,
forcing themselves
to find their own way through.

And here and there
along the way
a moment's triumph
brings them joy.

Friendship supports
and strengthens them
and love brings light
into the darkest hour.

Through all the thorns
they've struggled on
'til watchers praise
all they have done.

A friend gave me some words of Rabindranath Tagore. They had already been adapted and didn't altogether make sense (to me). So I've adapted them again!

Farewell my Friends

It was beautiful
as long as it lasted,
the journey of my life.
I have no regrets
whatsoever, save
the pain I leave behind,
those dear hearts
who love and care . . .

At every turning of my life
I came across good friends,
friends who stood by me,
whose strong arms held me up
when my strength let me down.

Farewell, farewell my friends.
I smile and bid you goodbye.
No. Shed no tears
for I need them not.
All I need is your smile.

'To live in the hearts of those we love is not to die.'

We none of us look forward to the actual business of dying but when it is over we slip into 'the care-free calm of death' knowing that life itself goes on and that something of our own life continues in the people we have loved and the things we have done. 'To live in the hearts of those we love is not to die.'

Pooh Sticks

They were playing Pooh sticks,
dropping them into the river
on one side of the bridge
and running to see
whose would pass beneath it first.

Their father watched a stick
carried by the current
of the stream
until it was out of sight.

'That's it,' he thought.
'We are dropped into the stream of life
and carried by the current,
who knows where.

Will our journey be cut short,
ending in a pile of driftwood
by the river bank,
or will we find our way,
twisting and turning, bumped and bruised,
until we end up lost in the sea?'

A Clockwork Toy

Sometimes it seems as though life is
rather like an old clockwork toy.

Fully wound it rushes through the early
years. But as the spring unwinds it
begins to slow until at last it comes
to a full stop. Its noise and movement
fall silent.

Childlike, we turn away and play with
other of our toys. But that is as it
should be. The best tribute we can
pay to those who have died is to

turn from death to life again and to
live our own lives positively and well.

The Question

The question is not
how far did you go
but what did you see and do
as you travelled on your journey.

Time

Time is not measured by the ticking of a clock
nor by the passing of the hours and days.
Time is measured in moments that are memorable,
in experiences that are precious to us.

So let us make the most of all our days,
living them out in warmth of friendship
and in depth of love –
spending each precious moment 'as if it were our last'.

Faced with the death of a young drug addict I sat with a family who found it desperately hard to find ANYTHING positive to say. But slowly, as we talked, a few precious memories began to emerge. When I got home I found myself writing:

Remember the Good Times

Remember the GOOD times,
remember only those.

There were good times you know,
smart times, cheerful times,
happy times when I was young
and life was good
and all the family was there.

Remember the good times,
remember only those.

Times of work and times of friendship,
times of love and times of courtship,
times of fun and times of laughter,
there were good times you know.

So forget the rest.
Just remember the good times,
remember only those.

Prayers and Blessings:

A religious ceremony will always contain prayers. A non-religious ceremony will often contain a period of silence 'for personal reflection and for those who wish to, to say their prayers.' That is absolutely right. *We should always seek to be as inclusive as possible.* But sometimes I am asked to go further than that – to lead prayers. Can it be done with a good conscience? Have a look at this which is introduced as 'a period of guided reflection or prayer':

> Let us honour those who live quietly and gently on the earth, charming the lives of others with the warmth of their kindness and the depth of their friendship.
>
> Using words of Paul in the New Testament, let us give thanks for a life shared and enjoyed: 'Whatever has been true, whatever honourable, whatever has been just, whatever pure, whatever has been lovely, whatever gracious; whatever there has been of excellence, anything worthy of praise', let us give thanks for these things.
>
> And may those who mourn find comfort, strength and support in the days ahead and a new strength of purpose to drive their own lives forward.

Here is something similar which is derived from a Christian book of services but adapted for universal use:

> In sorrow may we find consolation, support and strength; may we be grateful for all those good things we have been given; and may we draw closer to one another in friendship and in love.
>
> May each one of us become the strength of the weak, the comfort of the sorrowful, the friend of the lonely, and in so doing may we find and establish our own peace.

So much for prayer, what about blessings?

A religious ceremony will often end with a blessing and there are some very beautiful blessings in the Bible and in religious liturgies. These are often immensely comforting and reassuring.

A non-religious ceremony will not bless anybody in the name of a god, but it can end in positive hopes and good wishes, and sometimes religious blessings can be adapted. Here is an adaptation of words of Cardinal Newman:

> May human love and friendship support us all the day long until the shades lengthen and the evening comes; until the busy world is hushed, the fever of life is over and our work is done. Then may our lives move gently to their appointed end, blessed by safe lodging, rest and peace.

Among the poems there are expressions similar to this, which is Celtic:

> The peace of the running water to you,
> the peace of the flowing air to you,
> the peace of the quiet earth to you,
> the peace of the shining stars to you,
> and the love and the care of us all to you.

It is good to end a ceremony on a note of hope, good wishes and peace and I felt that it might be good to end this book in the same way so I'll finish with some closing words of my own:

> In days to come
>
> if we are troubled
> may we find peace;
>
> if we are depressed,
> may we find joy;
>
> and if we are lonely,
> may we find companionship and love.